CW00525279

Federal Gods

Dear Barbara,

Thank you so much

for coming.

Warmest wishes,

Clare

Palewell Press

Federal Gods

Clare Saponia

Federal Gods

First edition 2022 from Palewell Press, www.palewellpress.co.uk

Printed and bound in the UK

ISBN 978-1-911587-60-6

All Rights Reserved. Copyright © 2022. No part of this publication may be reproduced or transmitted in any form or by any means, without permission in writing from the author. The right of Clare Saponia to be identified as the author of this work has been asserted by her in accordance with the Copyright, Designs and Patents Act 1988

The cover design is Copyright © 2022 Camilla Reeve
The front cover photo shows children's shoes collected for war refugees at Keleti Railway Station on 7 September 2015 in Budapest, Hungary. In 2015, refugees were constantly passing through Hungary en route to Germany. The photo is Copyright © 2022 Istvan Csak / Shutterstock.com
The photo of Clare Saponia is Copyright © 2022 Clare Saponia

A CIP catalogue record for this title is available from the British Library.

Dedication

For a future us

Foreword

In 2015, Germany opened its doors to almost 1 million asylum seekers, most escaping war and persecution in various parts of the Middle East, Central Africa and Afghanistan, as well as economic migrants from the West Balkans and Eastern European countries.

Federal Gods is the sequel to *The Oranges of Revolution*, exploring the inevitable knock-on effect of civil wars, western intervention and imperialism on civilians, who risked their lives to reach safety in Europe, only to encounter new conflicts on arrival. The sometimes unsettling use of pronouns "you" and "us" throughout the collection is being deliberately spun to reflect an uncomfortably diverse range of opinions and reactions surfacing, not just in Germany, but indeed right across the continent with regard to immigration, religion and race.

I'd like you to come on this journey with me, with those I met, and allow me to set the scene through often dissonant, contradictory eyes: to pass the baton as narrator. I'd ask you to bear with me, to flow with the force of what was bubbling and visibly erupting in many neighbouring European countries, from Hungary and Holland to the UKIP-swayed UK, and at every level of society: From bricklayers and bankers to governing bodies. Whether native or foreign national. Because that's the voice driving the narration, as I navigate my way in and out of incongruous everyday settings: sometimes feeling strongly connected to the society I am living in, whilst at other times, detached, estranged or repelled. A foreigner myself.

On the evening of Friday 14th August 2015, at the height of the influx, the town hall in Berlin-Wilmersdorf was transformed into an emergency asylum home intended for up to 500 refugees. I was there that night with a load of other volunteers. It was over 33° C and people were arriving exhausted and dehydrated from often harrowing journeys.

Within weeks, the location was housing up to 1150 people. Many other disused sites were converted for accommodation purposes up and down the country and are still equally reliant on donations and local support. The strength of social engagement and solidarity in cities like Berlin at the peak of the crisis was nevertheless remarkable, proof that a country with a grim past has attempted to acknowledge and rework it. Arguably, the demolition of imperialist statues in the UK in spring 2020 suggests how urgently it needs to do the same.

Federal Gods documents a series of immigration stories, encounters, insights and harsh socio-political realities while volunteering at Wilmersdorf Town Hall. I started by helping out with the children but wanted to offer my language and teaching experience as a linguist. After all, migrants need communication skills as much food and shelter if they are to stand a chance of attaining residency. So, a few days after opening, I took a roll of paper into the canteen during lunch hour and started writing the alphabet on it. Within minutes, there was a crowd. They understood. *Teach us*, a couple said in broken English. *We need German.*

Together, we went in search of an unoccupied room. I wrote a time on the door and told the English speakers to spread the word. Around forty people turned up to the first session, a compote of nationalities, backgrounds, ages and education levels, some with none at all. We had neither furniture nor equipment, but you have to start somewhere.

A few days later, I ran into another woman who was doing the same. Word got around and the number of teaching volunteers, many retired, quickly grew. Before long, a timetable had been coordinated with rooms and lesson slots: German classes were happening pretty much all day every day, providing residents with a sense of purpose, progress, support and companionship despite huge uncertainties, bureaucratic stress, grief and untreated trauma.

Meanwhile on the other side of The Channel, the UK was scheming its own exodus. May 2015 saw Cameron secure his electoral victory on the promise of an EU referendum: a scorning of unity, cooperation and shared responsibility that was about to dislocate citizens, not only from their continent, but from their own communities, dividing families and friends. The ugly face of xenophobia and islamophobia lurked in the foreground, just as it did right across Europe – fear of the foreign and unfamiliar steering the UK's ship into hostile, protectionist waters and robbing the country's future of vital democratic freedoms.

Strikingly, the protest against the EU seemed to be stemming from the same source as the UK riots of 2011: anger at domestic government policy and a system that was failing people – from public healthcare, education and welfare meltdowns to military and economic prioritisation in the face of dwindling power on the global stage. The European Union, and perhaps more accurately, a strong, influential Germany, made the perfect whipping boy.

Living abroad, I was affected on various levels, practically and personally. Berlin was my home. I moved there in 2004. And suddenly I was confronting the question of whether I had the right to stay. I did. I say this with five years hindsight and gratitude to the state of Berlin that was quick to ensure settled UK citizens obtained permanent residency – and were not left stranded in uncertainty. I could not help noticing the irony of the situation, working with asylum seekers while my birthland rejects them, shuns Europe and displaces its own citizens.

For me, there was another element in the mix though: I had gravitated towards a city that paradoxically would have exiled me eighty years earlier. In fact, I obtained citizenship exactly eight decades after my dad's parents gained asylum in Britain – just four months before the UK officially left the European Union.

Another eleventh hour moment. A juxtaposition of events, so different and yet deeply interconnected when you get to nub of Brexit.

Despite initially moving to Berlin for adventure and creative reasons, really I couldn't have chosen a better place for confronting certain aspects of my family's past: the political and cultural hub responsible for dissolving their homelands. And I don't believe in coincidence. I chose. Just as I chose to study the German language and history, wanting to understand not only events that quite frankly defy rational thought, but also the fear of a nation that continues to flow through generations internationally, whether persecuted or not.

The undercurrents of suspicion and hate can be overwhelmingly potent, carried forward by our ancestors, and it's so easy to get caught up and consumed by them if we forget to stay present and look at the facts. In short, the country I've experienced first-hand and value today is not the one that drove my grandparents from their rural villages – despite concerning, ever-vibrant support for the right-wing AfD* party in many former East German states. Quite the opposite. Whilst UKIP was busy hoisting fearmongering posters of uprooted refugees, Angela Merkel had opened the gates to our Middle Eastern and African neighbours who were attempting to escape war, genocide, rape, starvation and inevitable human trafficking.

How many people have been left to drown in the Med and on other treacherous migration routes? The world could be doing so much more on a humanitarian level if it pulled together. As I write, Putin has escalated attacks on The Ukraine. Likewise, the political situation in Afghanistan has become critical again. And yet, in 2015, Afghans were being deported from Germany because the country was deemed safe next to Syria and Iraq. A bitter pill to swallow. Sure, Germany did a lot more than most, taking in over 2 million refugees between 2015-17, despite strong right-wing resistance, both domestically and Europe-wide. But who in their right mind would put their kids in a dodgy rubber dingy to "escape safety"?

Staying impartial is challenging. I've never known how to get involved "just a little bit", particularly where real people are concerned: *Menschen*. The German word is more exact. I mean, how do you *just* teach without discovering the person behind the exchange? Without building a bond? The moment you hear another person's story, you are connected by shared emotions or experiences. They become more than a passport number or casualty lumped together with a million others on the nine o'clock news.

However, by the end of 2015, I was essentially on the verge of burnout – not that I was prepared to admit it: trying to stay on the ball with work and keep a roof over my head, while teaching three hours a night on top, helping translate, and above all, worrying about people being shifted across the country, continent or worse still, deported without warning.

All this was my own choosing. Getting my group from ABC to streetwise spoken proficiency and keeping them safe had become the only thing that mattered. My day job felt comparatively meaningless, my leisure activities frivolous in the light of what was happening around me at the home. Although ultimately, I had zero sway over immigration issues higher up. The relocations took place in the early hours of the morning, no time for anyone to process the upheaval. I'd get messages from those who had vanished.

The collection documents my experiences more or less chronologically. Existentially, I was hitting meltdown, exhausted and erratic. It hurts to write this. I feel ashamed. Friends were telling me to reduce my hours or quit. But even the thought was tantamount to desertion and failure: betraying people I was emotionally attached to, and who stood to suffer more if they lost the right to stay. In the end, I had to leave. I was spent. And by far, not alone in that.

Federal Gods traces the highs and lows of life in transit. It confronts the arbitrary power of political elites, the economically motivated slanging matches between heads of state and those caught up in between. Most importantly, the poems aim to acknowledge the courage of individuals who have either lost everything or were willing to try anything for a life in safety:

the very human search for connection and acceptance in a sea of foreignness. For this is what unites us, liberates us, and allows us to grow.

* A full glossary of foreign and made-up words can be found at the back of the book.

"Have enough courage to trust love one more time and always one more time." **Maya Angelou**

1

You came in fat-packed cattle droves.

The pictures in the papers mirrored and multiplied you into fiction. Science fiction. You were the ones who saw Superman get dumped, Spiderman chuck in his climbing rope and Batman swap cloaks for Joker cards. You became grand master works carved out by vicious mathematicians, all puffed-up and roistering round after round with their scavenger media mob. You became carrion.
You became freaks
ogres
titans
cyclops
whopping great hysterical critter
hulking ruffians
and pythonic viruses.

You became disease. Overnight. Without knowing it. A flush of septic necessity. Feeding, sleeping, dreaming, seething. Streaming through the arteries of this land on national rail overdrive. No play for the fattening of gangly veins. The rot of history and contempt, as you nosedive through wounds, old and new, traumas tapered in at the heel. Boorish. Petulant. A viscid reminder of otherness and its tang of fear. Your fear. Your grandparents' fear. Every parent's fear. Anything but feel the dank drip-dripping about the cuff of their shoe. The long bleed of love that never sets. The clog of cultural goo.

They expected more evil than the evil in the devil himself, a peek behind curtains and TV screens as close as they're gonna get to the spangle of incomers hazing the streets, the nebula weave of unbleached skins, of ebony brows and beards: the compulsive fever of dread and gratitude warping the tone of their landscape. The hue of music, language, trust, loves, hates and tastes. The guttural hacking of voice recognition smarted to a mousse-padded muffle. The dyspraxic trill of literature scribed full-swing in reverse order like a lie detector graph gone ape. Bonkers. Lost the plot. The flood of knowledge gaps school never catered for. The tingle of foods that set mouths and minds aflame and put bland back on the map. All gone a tad too far. And never far enough. The tangos and salsas and rumbas that once screamed exotic, breakneck, bane of the waltz, now kneeling to the wield of tribal drums: bodies board-stiff yearn to bend from hips as if harnessed by a bad birth pill. Born by the wrong ocean. Wrong woman. Dance DNA sucked up somewhere down the Strait of Istanbul. And yet, there it goes the master race, straining to be at one with groove and its disciples. And feel. Yes feel. That thing. The burning foe of understanding. A melt of mental gullies the mind isn't ready for.

They come so close, their coffee reeks of suspicion. It seeps through filter upon filter: an acrid umber of unknowing, powdered fine as fishmeal beyond residue. But still there. Stagnating. Scourging in a bloat of pride. Far too proud to break rank and change a habit of a lifetime, as anomaly fills their line of sight.

And all since you came.

Before there was love. Real love. Coffee smelt of grilled almonds, kids sang to a medley of swastikas and sickles, and neighbours teetered between boot-licking and squealing. But at least they knew who they were dealing with. An otherness that was other but still the same. Same, same. The great eastern beast come for its prey. All knifing each other beneath a multi-coloured cape of guilt and indifference, the stitch-work half hanging out.

With you comes angst, awe, fright and funk. It's your all-weather mantle no number of caps, scarves and shrugs can mask. It oozes and throbs beyond body-length like an outer torso tattoo, a baggy etching chalked into a murder scene silhouette. Billowing greed. Billowing the trim of their bête noire baloney about lip and limb. Gaudy and gluttonous. Out to swallow you whole. Cos' guess what? There is no naked, airtight-sealed into that silhouette, ink-old as genetic code engraved back to front, back and front on our subconscious. Phobias cloned their way into books centuries before you could read, the fibres of everything we feel hosted by ancestral minds: faithless crimes rammed into laws and literature like the latest enlightenment footage. How much have we already seen?

Been there and back before in the blink of an eye, you know – every time we pace the way from home to bus to school to home. The dreams we have that have no endings, already dreamt by someone else

far, far off in other lands
just waiting for the next:

someone kinder and wiser, more willing to make good of them. Someone in it for the long haul.

For as long as life allows. An interest-free loan from mortality. An inch-thick stick of liquorice to suck on 'til their gums glow pooh-brown patent

from parrying. But we get off scot-free.

Did I mention fear?

Did I mention love?

Did I mention the fear of not being loved?

So easy to let gonads get in the way.

You were wondering where empathy started and finished. The TV showed red-carpet crowds awaiting you at Munich mainline. Flag-waving. Food-waving. The whole forecourt brimming with philanthropy. They cheer where you've come from. They cheer where you're going. They cheer what you've seen and what you've forgotten. They cheer the unknown. Faces they will never see again. Neighbours who never moved in. It has the thrill of Ascot: the marathon they watched but never ran. Alu-wrapped snacks and Evian thrust at you from every angle. Winter-weight jackets in the height of the heat. How long will this last, your first taste of us? Love and hugs just drooling on demand. Nothing like Greeks bearing gifts.

You swathe yourselves in the German flag like inside-out burritos. You're brave, I'm thinking. That drape'll stand between you and staying. It'll watch your every move, march against you on the streets: It'll turn history into fish story and be the last thing you see if you leave. The symbolism makes me heave. To you it's a magic cloak. It fends off hunger and war, brothers and sisters lost along the way. The fraudsters who bet you'd never make the finishing line. The fraudsters who knew there was no finishing line.

And you were hungrier for life than I have ever seen anyone. You made me hungrier for the life I wore like some invisible shroud I forgot I was wearing. You made me ask what flavour life was? You wanted a recipe I didn't have. A recipe I'm still inventing as I go. Our common ground. We move. We flow. We're never ready enough to eat. Too much salt and not enough spice. Like the cook's in love but longs for lust, a new day more thrilling than an old one. Run your tongue along your lips and they're ready for the next. Their taut tequila rims spin a glint of the dreams that will never leave you. They melt and dry and crack and melt again, over and over. I know, because mine do too.

We are serving instant black coffee to six-year-olds. They're nipple-trained, says the guy to my right. Safer than water back home, he shrugs. So now we have kids who could dance the night away, their folks wired all wrong from the same gut-scraping crap they've used to mind the first day of their new lives. Maybe remember it forever. The same sleeplessness no amount of coffee could prepare you for.

You'd sleep on the spot if they let you.

And you came in spates through the night, waiting for names and numbers to be called, waiting for signs or something you understand beyond passports and stamps and surnames your hosts cannot say. For someone to tell you something – not just *warten Sie bitte. Warten. Wir bitten um Geduld.**

They tell you sleep cannot happen yet. Everything has its order, from people to postcodes, photos to food. Every second of your day is now cinched by queues. Sculpted by times and dates and desk numbers with more letters than numbers. Doors and hearts that close beyond your groove. Bells and buzzers that have the final say, while the little people play prophet with pensions to swell. Civil servants demoted to gods with no time for real world deeds. You see eagles everywhere, tattooed to buildings and costumes and paperwork you can't read. The cult you want to join, but have neither keys nor clues.

They feed candy to your kids to kill time. To wash down the caffeine they've caned like Christmas-cold turkeys, all tanked up on E this and that. Sugar surging their state of never-sleep, the neverending game of never landing. Milka and football forever, it seems.

Reality we can all cope with.

You feel the cold in the hours after sundown, limbs sore from the stone-gravelled seating you can no longer sit on. Waiting for existence to start. Rammed like heifers to the left-hand side of the yard. Only kids allowed to be kids.

You look for a ball to batter. To beat back the cold excreted from our raven sky. The stars too far away to matter. The stars so far away, you wish harder. All the extra clothes you should've brought. Could've carried. Instead of opening your palms to the grace of strangers.

2

The beds arrive.

This is an event.

This is happening.

More wow than you can imagine.

More hope than you can handle.

They have scheduled sleep. It arrives in pieces, trucks storming the quad, spewing metal parts from person to person, the untrained chain gang we are. Poles and slats and springs pouring from hand to hand, never touching the ground. People stop to watch: a movie in the making. From boxes to beams, this is love in motion picture. Massive great crates of the stuff: pillows and throws, sweaters and soap, sanitary stuff from public pockets that won't last the week. Ratted mattresses – but not enough to go round.

You get three blankets instead.

I wanted more for you. But who are you with another man's shirt on your back?

Your wife speaks for you. She asks me questions I can't answer, one after the other in a spitfire of ruptured English. A gust of needs evaporating before her eyes as people pour in

18

by the bus-load: 16, 37, 52, 143, 178. The forecourt inflates fortyfold. Familiarity contained to a ring on your finger, a photo in your purse, that scarf round your neck; voices you've seared into your memory. Voices you wish you had here. Promises you wish you'd delivered.

3

The room multiplies within minutes. Three becomes twelve, becomes twenty-five, becomes forty-five, chairs a luxury we don't have. Just an overlap of flesh and bone twinging side by side. Just the hungry and restless looking to fill their time with something beyond strife and sinking dinghies, where hot and cold, love and pain mean the same in any language.

The attendance list hanging on the wall is empty. No one knows enough German to realise it's a list: that the land they've signed up for demands names on just about everything. You have to choose your lists

carefully, consider the pros and cons of wiring desires in print. Cos the wrong one could mean out.
       Out of sight.
              Out of mind.
Tacky black question mark in a system that's both prison and passport to your future before you commit, a hem of catalysts and cocktails.

I awake screaming, monstrous reams of figures gushing into the air like rogue computer coding. From registered arrival dates to birth and expiry rates, this is how we lose track of love. This is how we force-feed amnesia to a state of bulimic

greed. Have I bitten off more than I can chew?

The reasons merge now. The reasons have changed. I increase my hours. My input. My conscience now bigger than the fuse of my ego. And now the fear that it'll all go pop. I watch everything else around me deflate, from income to fun. Voices, not my own, tell me to stop. But I can't. 'Cause stop is failure. Stop is fraud and desertion. Stop is my guilt for having other goals. Stop is an admission that this will never stop, when in fact, it's only just got started.

4

Zaid

I ask your date of birth. Not out of nosiness...
Though I want to know. Too. Just not here.
Here, I'm probing your feel for figures, how you
translate life from one calendar to the next: a
parallel universe that says the same but
doesn't. I want to say welcome to the land of
numbers. There're cardinal combos and prime
puzzles everywhere you turn. They tell you
where to go, when to go and who to see. They
tell you if you've won or lost. If you're in the red
or black. Or in the doghouse. They tell you if
you're allowed to live or die. And they make
great tattoos that thrive in the afterlife. Better
than letters.

You have your own one. You become a
snowflake. But we could find you in a blizzard if
we had to, branded under foot or birch.
Browned beneath the weight of newer flakes.
Your number goes nowhere without you.

You're an algorithm only we can track. We
create it, use it, shift, juggle or reproduce it. We
shear and shed our favourites to fit the bill. You
take it or leave it of your own free will. You show
me this stamp and that. You point to signs and
seals that prove you were hatched, and so far
from our linden soil. We don't want to split hairs.
All that time spent eating real limes, as it turns

out.

As it turns out, you've seen more with your age than I have. You've had one less spin around the sun, a dozen fewer visits from the moon. You've crossed continents with more hope than hardware in hand. Your lifepath wanted other things for you. You wear your guts inside out, dependent on my tongue and my willingness to share it with you. A code that will make or break. And yet, I feel like a child next to you playing pundit, choosing who can join in our game, who will love or hate their new landspeople.

I decide.

I decide not to tell you I'm not German. Not yet. The woman writing this now has an eagle manning every page of her pass. It watches over her moves, all the flights to and from, the last-minute lapses and careless no-shows. It doesn't miss a trick. Doesn't die. Digital forever is what she is now. Every inch of her past spreadeagled from cover to cover. Never more grateful for the right order of letters and numbers. The skirting of roads she can't tread anymore. How much longer can she say: I'm not Stiller?

The eagle keeps good and bad books. But I've learnt to play the role well with my copper-blond locks and Teutonic tone: Speaking my mind. Pausing in all the right places. Choosing

Pumpernickel over Toastbrot*. This ploy and
that to keep the non-native tight under wraps.
You'll see Zaid. You'll do the same, if they let
you stay.

5

Intesar

Blood bonds me with your wife. We're wired differently, we women. The moon in the month feeds us the same sense of time you could never know. Circles of love and loss that aren't tied to the lands we live in. Circles we share, even in ignorance. We're never strangers, gel like spilt juice to one another, molecule by molecule. Wasps like us all.

And I like you too, Intesar.

We touch each other with arms and eyes. You're smart. Smarter than the thirty men in the room who can barely read in their own tongue. Your mouth more nimble to the rumple of new sounds. Your memory more agile. I watch you lap it all up and spit it back through your jowls

the very next day

and the next. Neither tired nor scared of error. Nothing left to lose but fear. And you left that two thousand miles away.

Instead you brought bravery and a heart, brains bound in polyimide film like you were bolting from Oz in the freeze. No lion or tin-man in tow. And I realise you're more than just an elephant in the room here. Standing where you stand. Saying what you say at the top of my class. You

are power. You are pressure. You have something the others don't. Because you're a woman.

6

Zaid

Yeah, she's sharp, you nod, trying not to smile,
Intesar hiding all she knows, but answering this
question and that. Sifting triple figures in her
head for a laugh. Back home, for a living. She
jostles sums and signs, your sidekick: has titles
and letters after her name. Though here, she's
just she. I hear the pride in your voice as you
reveal her, your love locked into that hulking
glottal stop I struggle to get my lips round.
Never mind my tonsils.

Her brains boost you, I can tell – on the run from
a war you couldn't win on love alone. Not there.
Love was leaving it behind. Leaving elders and
minors too old or little for the road you took.
They hold the fort you call home

in your heart. They have a closet strength you'd
never seen, a fight you were tired of fighting,
trying to tend to the next generation. *You
couldn't stay! You couldn't stay!* You hold my
wrists. Your eyes turned to molten cacao as
you tell me this. You speak for you both. You
said there were lies hatching manifold as
stillborns, grifters ripped and sliced from
silence. And now no one picks up the phone.

You tell me about your inner war, your skirmish
with Mr C and his vicious henchmen, those

sober giblets and naïve bowels you've fought tooth and nail for. You say you were operated. You say, you've beaten him back, that you seem to be winning, for now. And five years on I'm wondering too. You raise your shirt,

shameless,

to Julia and me – as if we wouldn't believe you. We look, trying not to stare, Intesar shrugging and mumbling words to keep the evil eye at bay: the fat, ragged weave descending your gut like a rhubarb worm, a Victorian teddy torn in two. The worm dives beneath your belt, sneak preview not for class. I sense the length of its stride, its all-knowing grasp of old worries and wounds, the world you want to change, a thwart of slimy lilac fisting out of the husk of you. Udon noodle funnelling through your rind. The lull

before the storm.

You repeat *you're ok*. Just a check-up, you claim. We both know the Staat[1] has a strong distaste for sick people: that the weak suffer more from deportation. That the bolshie, fruitful and krank[2] can find themselves on the next boat back, quick as kid shits. And neither of us can face that.

It seems crucial to you to convince me, Zaid. Can't you tell I am? Batting for your team. Flanking at your side. I'm with you all the way. It's just the system I can't rewrite. And I'm

watching the strain in your jaw, muscles fraught
from the pidgin English you still favour to
Deutsch, mouthing with pineapple bark
between your jowls. Your wife is watching too,
squinting at words she can only guess at.
Waiting for footnotes. Waiting for real hopes.
Wondering why Julia is wincing at the front of
you. She's squeamish. It's as simple as that:
the purple viper you forget to veil in your fear,
flaunting your paunch for all to see.

I sign to lower your shirt. There's no mission to
win with us. No test to pass or act to play. We
want you well, Zaid. We want you both well. We
want the love from your wife to be enough

to live on.

And when I close my lids now, I can still see
that scar dangling in front of my third eye: a
haggard braid, tiptoeing into the unknown.

We take you aside after class. A mix of warmth
and shame skids across your greyish mug.
You've tried to explain. Once. Twice. The guys
at the front desk not concerned, you say. *You're
healed*, they say. Healed. *You're living proof.*
Your story not grim enough. Pain not big
enough. You left out the words death and dying,
they say. *Remission's not a condition.*
Remission's more taxing than the sick to the
State, a public health bill in the making.

There's no budget for you. There's no budget

for us either. But the system's not stacked to help unless you're stiff on arrival. The system likes black and white, dead or alive. The system wants to know since when, how long, dates and stats and stamps from your doc. *Auf Deutsch*[3] of course. The system wants names of meds and dose, your height and weight and blood count. It wants to know the pump of your heart at a standstill, both pulse and pressure on a high. It wants your pooh colour and sugar strain, the whats and whys to how they've changed. Failed. Fully recovered. The system doesn't get unfinished stories. It notes how quick your hair's grown back.

You say you're a disease waiting to happen. Again. The second you look away. The second your concentration lapses, along comes Mr C and canes your complacent arse. I observe your juggling eyes. The whole thing is just so damn bloodless, belated portions of bad egg gassing round your new home like karma's pissed with you. Shoals of cops standing between you and certainty, their purpose taut as oxtail, their logic lost to the wind, like you've sped across the lights and left your brakes on. You lean in closer. You don't want the gods to hear. Not the kind who need dates and stamps. But you can't find the way.

7

I ask where Intesar is.

Sad, you say, shaking your head in oval hoops.
You mean upset, depressed, fucking miserable
but palm me the first word that springs to mind.
Maybe you're being restrained, a diplomat and
a gentleman. Maybe it really is the only word in
your mind right now, you and that trickster
sickness that's itching to have its way.

You got bullied in line, you say. Browbeaten by
the local hotshot throwing his weight about the
joint. The new boy in town. The sore loser and
green-eyed one, who's never gonna get a girl
like that. Not here. Maybe not anywhere. Bad
food bringing out the beast in the boy, the way
he claims his prey like tarred mutton
medallions.

It's ugly. I'm sorry you have to see this. I'm sorry
you have to live here. I'm sorry I can't do
anything about this and make him go away. I'm
sorry I can't stop saying sorry. I catch myself
doing this a lot of late. You must be wondering
what it means. You must be wishing you'd
never put the words *help* and *me* together in the
same sentence. And I wish I could take you
both in. Well away from here and the hazards
of unclean hands. But I can't. Daren't share my
cohabited dive with more than mice. And you're
too polite to ask.

The people here aren't good, you say, dissecting The Levant in a way I have no right to ascertain. Though I see how sensitive you are, your grasp far exceeding my three words of Arabic: the blokes beating each other up over single birds, the assaults and rapes and silenced woes, the people who vanish in the night to who knows where. The words I can only nod to.

I trust my body to do the sifting. I have to. Guys hang outside the classrooms, hover round stairways and night-time foyers I need to pass: men who spit and hiss and swear when they feel like it. But I don't have to live here. These are the men you mean, Zaid: the ones pestering your wife, cussing your face. These are the men she's sad about, ashamed for. Louts who buy lasses ten-a-penny at market, the way they haggle over herds, wholesale-style. You have nothing in common but language and loss. Not even how you got here: on and off a plane in four hours.

There were no dealers and dodgy dinghies. And you know they know. You know they smell wealth like bloodhounds to bones, though your make-do beds are no more comfy than theirs.

You don't know men like this back home. Men like this don't even work for you, jealous of the life you had, the wife you have: the woman you can love and hold at night, when our northern air gets cold and other arms lie bare. You understand this. It always comes down to sex. As if being slit from kin weren't enough. No umbilical cord to your past and none to your future without a bedfellow by your side. And stranded is what they are in more ways than

one.

You're ashamed for them, you say. For their conduct as guest in my country. For the country you think is mine. You've thought this through more than I have.

8

Black Hole on the Wall

Diced-up. Sacrosanct. Calcification of ideas.
Otherwise spelling death in their lucid,
smashed-up chalk fodder form.

Not a board.

Not a 2-D ban on life
and discovery and call-
girl-style illegitimacy.

Not plain, flat or flaccid
but a bottomless microcosm,
a history of blackboards
bringing the past

to the present,

hands on cobbles
as if I'm down there
with them.

9

Are you the teacher? she squints, digesting how I've waltzed in and out for weeks, silent with purpose, suffusing the access point under her nose. Her label throws me – as if I'm the only one crafting sovereign classes, scrawling on walls I haven't signed for. My cover is blown, the machine more consumed by who I am than what I do. Maria smiles. Maria just wants a simple yes from me and then everything can push on as planned. I teach, I say, smirking at the question she hasn't asked. She frowns, people needling her about staff she knows nothing about. Who, I prod? She waves a vague hand shaman-style and hints at the hundreds hostelled around us. Her index digit darts past Kochar and relief kicks in as he catches my eye. He's still here. Still illiterate. Still intending to try his luck on the farraged gut of my birth isle – if the Bundesarmee doesn't get there first. And then one day,

he'll be gone. Either by choice or not.

And there'll be nothing more I can do than let go and move on.

10

Thirty-five butts carpet the floor of our hub. The room's a shell. A heave of expectation and so little understanding.

I hoped *eins, zwei, drei* might be enough to turn off the hate tap for an hour or two. Momentarily distract you from the war paths crossed in your minds, in the quad and canteen and the roads that burn already, curb for curb, in the many days between. I hoped for tabula rasa. I hoped the shaky tatters of German grammar might just tear you from the shreds of your past: the flesh of your grudge. You have no reason to trust. Neither me nor your neighbours here, crouched knee to knee in the yolk of our cage. You have histories I cannot heal with *haben und sein** and present perfect tenses that have nothing much to do with the present. You've already sniffed out your enemies in the room. You throw daggers at each other when my back is turned. You wait for each other to fail from one to ten. And I can't teach you the words for mother and father, brother and sister without making you cry.

Where's this leading if we can't all be friends?

I plaster the lemon-sour walls with stripped recycled sheets I've dug out of storerooms, charity shops and waning home supplies: defeated scrap pads that have turmericked at the corners over time, now bundled beneath cheap tapes and Blu Tack imitations that take the wallpaper with them when they fall. Here, we're all set for landslides: intros overlapping body parts, body parts overlapping climatic spheres, sporting status and case ending chaos stashed under numbers. Just never enough nominative in the mix, no matter how much you dumb down dative or act out accusative: Pictures and pie charts, grid upon grid plotting the progress of tongues, one step closer to integration. One line closer to work and friends and the scent of residence. Maybe even permanence. If that counts for anything anymore – with everywhere and -one you have been between. All those skins you are still trying to shed, if resistance doesn't get in the

way.

Here, you're about as far from permanence as you could get. There are no boards with fancy markers, no chairs or tables or even bricks for cushions. There are no clocks on the walls to note when we start and close. Intuition has brought us there. All of us. Though you have travelled further. And intuition tells us when to

end.

Nikro springs up and down on the spot cursing all Iraqis. He's spitting little bits of flinted rage all over the place, while the others just watch or nod to our nine o'clock now show. A Balkan batch swaps internal squirms across the room, mother to child to newfound friends and back again, discomfort growing with every glance, the whole ruckus fucked in translation. There are no Iraqis in here. There never were – An outcome I had no hand in long before I set foot in this den, my blistered crew arranging itself in organic rank and file, from felony to foe, tolerance to treason. And I'm trying not to stand too far to the left or right in these sullen camps of code I'll never be part of.

Officially, I'm not here of course. Officially, I'm Clara, who the fuck is Clara, who comes and goes like the wind four nights a week leaving a prowl of language, mutant ivy-creeping up and down the walls. Officially, there's someone who signs herself in and out with neither pass nor right to be there, just the bland purpose of Deutsch, Deutsch and more Deutsch. But no more, no less. No curriculum. No qualifications. No boss to call the shots. And nobody gave a toss about the yolky larynx of learning until the day they thought to fling a lick of paint, don it with blackboard and benches in return for clout I don't do deals with. I bring language, not bureaucracy. And I feel the tightening of something that started as goodwill, an up-front share and rake of skill: to have them talking in three tenses by Christmas. And I make promises to myself even I can't keep in the euphoria of pleated needs that change in months to pass.

The room is etched a little more into life by the

day. And Julia is part of that. Julia is the only one who's met this merry troop, witnessed how they vanish by the week; displaced, dodging authorities who seek to displace, determined yet drifting from place to place. Another land. Another ocean. A series of trucks and containers and four-by-four boots, a sway of undercarriage and tyre racks. We know. They message us from the shaft of Calais, tucked up in tombs goodness knows where. They want to be friends forever caught between crater and abyss – unremitting dimples on the solar plexus of philanthropy.

Kochar dreams of Scotland, the outer skirting of the Outer Hebrides his skin would crumple under if he actually got there. He sends us porn photos and phallicised memes from the other side of the docks in the hope of keeping in touch. He doesn't listen to the red-flag warnings of Farrage's fiends, the wrangle of unkempt lies on the wrong side of the Wirral. The ones flaring back and forth on soap-box banter: not against the EU – but against YOU, the flume of counties kipped full-kilter into partisan freight. This is twenty-first century roulette rollocked to buggery by the pitch of weighted dice, a welcome gesture girdled by the naïve skew of urgency. It tick-tocks inside, a time bomb nagging you north from a dent in your angst, never knowing when to stop, when enough is enough – because landing is the picture others have painted for you.

And like that, he was gone. This is how they go. Some of them. One quick blink and the journey goes on without you. A journey you played no more than cabin crew to, handing over coffee, handing out directions. And then they're off. You: lamppost to a Yorkshire terrier trying to find its way home. And you've seen so many terriers since summer stormed on by, boarding trains they had not meant to catch.

It's ok to be a lamppost. It's ok to be in transit. And this pound we're in moves faster than any train I've ever taken, turnover trowelled by the day and hour: grown-ups guided in, youths escorted out. Sucked five hundred miles south of the track. And I cannot keep track.

They don't all come to learn. They come to escape the boredom of each other, the spouses and kin they're cooped up with day and night. The turf wars and tribal conflicts that have followed them across the Med to the peevish walkways of Wilmersdorfed suburbia. Some are out to get each other. To finish what was started in unvoiced towns and villages, a slide of benchmarks blown sideways off the map, a hoist of housing and school descended into smidgens. A future of grain and mite with love: mere morsels of vicious smithereens.

Some see sisters and wives and dazzlingly bright green cards in Julia and me, golden-maned goddesses leaping about in the soot of trench warfare, testing the vestige of someone else's business we just happen to land ourselves in.

We chose. Don't get me wrong. There's just so much of what we chose that we wouldn't have chosen. For us or anyone. The quicksand of it, nibbling on milestones for elevenses, making chasms out of castles. How did we get caught up in that, trading clarity for a cleft mesh of insider knowledge, our vantage points caving by the week, inch for inch?

Nikro claims all Iraqis here are ISIS fry. He balks at the Balkans and flouts the Afghans. He relegates Senegal, pooh-poohs Cameroon and ejects Ethiopia on ethical grounds. From Ghana to Mali, through Egypt and Turkey, has there ever been a good time to look for a better life?

The competition stinks. The rest are rot, he scoffs: a wasteland of pawned favours kneaded into the dough of plenty. Foul, he says: fucking foul fools with badder than bad intentions. His fear is louder than his rant, his fear aching and weeping like a chorus of dislocated corpuscles to the thud of our Bundesbogeymen. For Nikro, Iraq is just a plague on the other side of god, the hobgoblin of bane that tags his every move, his thoughts and dreams and memories trifling with the obscene, whenever the place is furthest,

but couldn't be nearer.

So, there's a bandwagon to jump on, it seems. He's looking for passengers and partisans, a thick drive of bile beyond the bend of disaster. The flintish lure of defiance in his speak. Intellectual for a mile that others wouldn't walk alone. But this is how the heartsick cave in care, U-turn on values once grounded in the vernacular. Dependent on pain to revive a sense of home. Self-harmers wilt to a steer of kindness that's bound to kill when spun too far from rage. This is how browbeaten looks more mighty than it is.

I'm not sure they see the pitfalls, the sperm of trauma pebbled-dashed along each fork in the road, sorry as proud flesh. Grown men doped up on amphetamines, neurotic as you like. They label us from worst to bad, a bar chart of trolls tagged to the promises we make and fail to keep, crushed beneath a rule of thumb.

There are several. The unsaid system is fissioned into five tracts of Arabic, a sprig of Farsi and pinch of Albanian, an alloy of another fifty shaping their own. All this hums within bird's eye view, the feast of dialect our eagle's tone-deaf to: the deals that get agreed over mouldy cheese, the laws no state can account for.

Nikro fears for his name: the peasants, farmers and faithless opportunists who'll wreck his cred before he even hits registration; scars woven from cheek to chin and back like fake tattoos that don't belong to him. A whiff of New Year's nonsense you had nothing to do with. And suddenly you're less welcome than you once were, lumped in with lechery – because it's the bad guys they remember first. The ones who reaffirm familiar fears; who drag a trail of dread and phobia about, creased as a kid's security blanket. You can smell it coming, can't you Nikro? Like Zaid. Like Intesar and Bora. Blacksheeped overnight by the bugbear of reason, until only clichés count.

Let's be frank: It always comes down to Formula One versus Formula Three. And there's just never enough size or speed to get us where we want to be. Hell is not the others, but a dangle of white inferiority. Horror that you'd be better in bed. That your wombs might welcome love more than our own. That the future cares more about conception than deception. And that your kind of love could mean the extinction of us.

You bring more men too and we've done the maths. Behind the solitude and scorn is both silence and violence. The rage we grow with not enough girls to go round, the envy and hate always on tap. So much man-hate in the history of humans and no word for it. Just wasted, rejected, thrown to the battlefields: no use to the future of the family, the pollination of the nation. The tide of hormones leaves our pride in shrivelled tatters: this and that we just hadn't noticed before. Answers so close they were glaring us in the face on the far side of clarity. Not everything can be cleaved into sink or swim: matter of fact with all fact removed. When will we stop chasing clichés that have more power than people?

11

Zaid & Intesar

It's hard not to send out fear when you look into the phobic eyes of others. How do you learn to do that? How do you not think terrorist when you run into shards of ice blue gaze, melt into the image spammed to your brow faster than birdshit?

You ask for my number. You sense something we both don't know, when you pull out a pen, and I've no need to question why. For now, the enclaves of gangs are enough, the funk of nationalist nobodies throwing their weight about, nasty as they come. Until now,

I've wildly defended my right to be unreachable. Until today, I've never really left my phone on at night. Just select moments for poorly parents or pals launching into labour, radioactive Martians frazzling their way through the night, nothing better to do than throw raves in my sleep. A

light in the room that never goes out. On the lookout. Always on the lookout. As if a reel of digits could turn ill-fate around. How much of your impulse was precaution – and how much, prediction? These are the questions no one else can answer for you. Though we both hope

you haven't asked for something you can't take

back. I wonder where you're headed, at your age. At our age. Still no kids in tow between war and inner wrangles you couldn't have planned for. I wonder if there were kids you couldn't shield but mask my curiosity: think of anything

I can do to get you out of this dive.

12

On the twenty-ninth of the ninth it rang twice.
Twice more than I wanted. A number I didn't
know. A number I knew without needing to
know what I didn't. I just knew, knowing that
knowing couldn't help, my heart crazed with
mania. My heart: rattling full-fisted against the
cages of my chest – for the bounce and bend
of a system I have no access to. Unknowledge
is such a saintly tool. And I wish I could unknow

what I don't know, blindfold the unbearable.

Unable to bear.

Unable to run. So, I do the next best thing and
just stare at it, at the scud of hope spindling out
of it, spit for spit, the future set in motion long
before we are ready for it. And we'd give
anything to know which god was put in charge
here, moving you on 'cos your birthday bingo
call came through, slapdash as Vietnam
draftings. And now, you're shifted, elapsed,
slung-shot somewhere east of the most
easternest Kommune*, where too many white
men have been left hanging for too long

and they don't know who to blame first.

It's always the smart ones who get moved.
Maybe you've noticed? The way these gods
hedge bets on survival stats, as if natural
selection could do a better job when someone's

due to take the whack for this.

Rumour has it you can't stay where you register first. I wish we'd known. I wish you'd booked to Freiburg before bowing to the unremitting trawl of Deutsche Bahn, the thought of some uncivil servant tossing darts at a map with both eyes

shut.

I probe you by sms, the missed calls and data breach I'd have normally condemned to junk by now, were my gut not running the show. *We miss you*, you write the next day.

I ask if you're ok, if you need help. I ask how and what, where and why. I ask these questions all the time of late. But these mean more. You say they came in the night like they always do and chucked you on a train to Eisenberg: a veteran railway net that knows its way round the nation better than anyone when it comes to shifting refugees. A genetic gift left dozing over the decades, slick as sleeping beauty, now hosting night raids on tap. I awake

to a trippy giddiness, icicles dribbling barbs of anguish down my spine, polka-dot-poking through the hunch of my hood. A crossbar of rill

dissecting the undercurrent of

sleep.

Dreams were racing wild all night. Dreams were stringing me along, flashing their little secrets now and then like juiced-up poets. And there I was, fighting to defy gravity. Burying myself 'til ten. 'Til that text snapped me out of it.

I feed Eisenberg to Google and it spits back Rheinland-Pfalz. I feel Zaid frown when I mention Westdeutschland and *good that he's there*. I can feel him frown down the phone, my relief jumping guns that are more than semi-loaded. Google overlooks the other Eisenberg, a pin-drop of a postage stamp squat duskily in the backwaters of Jena.

He asks what it's like there, mind open as a mussel with its soul hanging out. I don't know how much truth is too much. Living in fear is no better than living in fog. *Never been*, I say in the end, suggesting he keeps his eyes as open as his mind, and that I'm just a phone call away. My words feel bigger than I am.

13

The blurb between Bundesländer* sucks and I feel impotent, spoilt sat here in some cinema, whilst you've been sent to the Blyton-bound burg of Iron Mountain. And I can't bring you back.

I'm barely watching the film in fact, my thoughts sounding dud off the walls of my skull every time I scout for a lead. Somewhere between Berlin and Eisenberg.

I'm crap conversation tonight too. And it's not inertia. I'm neither idle nor inactive. But the banality of this ballgame sickens and I'm clearly better off in dream, a little further from Kafka castles, a little closer to Böll-esque clowns. I can hear the dull out-of-tune thump of ill-suited boots pounding the arse end of the world, the echo of weary infant groans and luggage clatter pummelling the cobbles in turn. I hear the wails for unmourned mothers. I smell the sour, ferrous twang in a downwind sneeze, spy the cocky hilltop buzzards playing hero through the breeze, handgliding on an upthrust of russet-skinned dust, a curtain of metallic voices swung wildly to
ebb

       and

         flow.

The voices become thinner, more diaphanous the further up we go, and even iron smelts to the fold of edifice, always beaten back in the prelude to silence.

There's the trick:

sucking up lungs between happy Saturn rings in our range. High above sea level. Just a fishy dust miracle. But the whole hula-hooping thing has wings. It turns heads. It lops off heads. It cleaves through belly, breast and womb. Welcome. Welcome. As long as you don't stay. And there's only one way down.

I wake up choking, skull cooped between pillow and frame with tissues I planted there weeks ago in my yawn – now returning from the feats of night. There are five of them, duck-tailed origami gulls flaunting the brink of yoga with their shifty grins. I crush them a bit tighter 'til something brittle snaps with the alacrity of finger bone and my affection breeds each into two and a half birds. The half: a one-shot birth, still waiting

to hatch.

The moisture of morning's smoke swarms my hive. A single creek of sweat carves out its path

slowly

surreptitiously

staging a bleed from far-left blade to bottomest ribcage, swamp of needs in the small of my back. I glide an index down my spine, a kebab skewer of rinsed crabapples beneath the dough of rind, oil and acid trying to get on in the folds of my husk. Is this middle age? What age do my dreams take me to? How many time zones and grey zones have I crossed? And how much of this do I manage not to judge?

There's more taboo than I'd like. I feel this in the chill of my damp sheath, the sweet, tacky remains of an inner rant I can't contain, like a rogue boar on rebound. I rely on a simple mingle, body-goddessing not to get old amid the race for infertility. It's not as easy as it looks. There are booby traps all over the place. But I can feel the pull, the tang of something more thrilling stirred up on tenterhooks, snippet by snippet, once biology has got bored.

I've felt the pull since I first started slinging eggs to a carefree offbeat umpteen moons ago: the way they spin willy-nilly against the thrash of gravity. But creeping, always creeping up on me in pink silk slippers

until one day they won't.

And maybe we'll both be laughing once we stop freaking each other out in the stunt of dream.

For now, my body has become a stranger to me, the Eisenberg of flesh I haven't learned to reckon with: big, fat knowledge gaps I try to seal with temporary thinking.

Zaid,

it's like our two Eisenbergs have bloated since we spoke, fake and fern-decked three hundred miles apart, stark as Madonna bras, and yet so far from anything close to an immaculate collection. I notice how Eisenberg becomes less of a name, a team of anonymous chimneys, stone-boned, smoking themselves

to infertility.

Stop.

I hear a voice in my head, the me of fifteen years' shier and Brussels-bound, more café and cognac than I could handle. More autism than I knew what to do with. Just a hearth of nicotine reading into the future.

14

That year, I missed my flight, hiked halfway across Europe on a string of trains to get home: to host the New Year's Eve we'd planned. I penetrated three national borders on one pass, changed pesetas into this franc and that to get fed. To get back before you. Going with the migrant flow.

My passport was never alien enough to spurn my groove. One glimpse of EU script and the guard slaps it into my palm, subtle, snide, same routine over and over with us white ones. Sudan and Senegal do a much better job at quelling his yawn. Sadism on tap. And most of them don't make it past Nîmes. The captions

come and go

over the years. Never had we expected to be part of them, our bedrock dismembered, right by right, in the Blitz of Brexit. All those crossings we've made, rivers and roads and a trim of ocean, just to reach us: wise-arse blared across the windshield. Though you opted out of the whole shebang, took a left turn and left again

before anyone could take it from you. I guess we both did in our own way, wreaking havoc on the fringe of time like we had forever. I remember every second on the dance floor that night. I beat you by barely two hours back to Brussels, blood brother and sister swapping poisons and more

with forty percent in our veins.

You ring and write I don't know who. He said he
found fifty missed calls the next day from his
wasted bro, blotting out all the vibes in the
room. I guess the network was just shit back
then. Lucky to have one. And you remember
nothing of what happened after that point. You
phoning Neptune. Me dancing with anyone who

could keep up. Both of us managing fun on our
own terms. Both of us healing insecurities that
had long gone by twenty-fifteen, making up the
rules as we go along. And little do we know that
you'll cave, take a sharp dive out of life a year
from now, whilst I spend my weeks with
strangers, torn between Eisenbergs.

15

At the welcome gate, they strapped barbed wire
about your savvy hands, fingers that are trained
to perform tucks and twists on precious organ
grind in their sleep like they're buckling shoes,
carving out squamous malware, pin and bolt, as
they were born to:

fingers that have spent more time inside other
people's bodies than your own.

Fingers that have stood between life and death
awaiting orders from above.

Orders that now come from the Home Office,
Job Centre, Department for Work and
Pensions: stay low, keep your eyes to the
ground, don't get too comfortable with the deft
sweep of your doctor's wherewithal. It's
dependents, not docs, they want: a whole hush
of airheads, not public service saints, makes
them so much easier to send packing. Your
degrees

don't count.

Your skills, compassion and acumen

don't count.

You,

YOU,

with that spotless track record

within earshot,

go stand in line.

16

The man with Tourette's takes his pew on a
stone wall opposite the café, cussing gypsies,
cussing capitalism, cussing the AfD[1] down to
size. *Fressen! Ficken! Fertig!*[2] he roars,
spewing his love of hate into the cold October
sun. He changes character every five minutes,
aiming his rant at those who are trying hardest
not to notice. And of course, you can't not
notice. All you can do is savour the silence
between blusters, his pauses like full-body
rubs. My chest is buzzing from his tirade at ten
a.m., the way he curses war and conflict, but
creates his own among the oblivious hip,
hitched up there on his Speaker's Corner.
Retching on demons. I wonder what he'd do,
Zaid, if you stood in front of him. Just stood and
said nothing.

I wonder which box you'd fit into, which evil
you'd bring to his world; neither gypsy, German
nor Jew. I wonder how many more of his type
you'll meet along the way, what your best line
of defence against jihadist jibes might be

from bishop to knight

and castle to king

and you know from the stillness in my glance
that I mean it when I say *watch out, take care*
well before you are gone. You showed me the
dampness of your sockets. I saw them drip two-

time to the peals of change you can't control.
Like a real man. And suddenly it is five years
on.

17

Amina

You'd let me flash picture cards at you for hours
hungry for: words
                    numbers
                    knowledge
                    and nonsense.

You don't know that others can quash this with
the same: words
                    numbers
                    knowledge
                    and nonsense

others high up: more than several times your
age because if you learn, you can stay. If you
speak, you can query, call them out when push
comes to shove. But they can't curb your
curiosity, muzzle the smarts that help you sift
photos and scribbles at six. They can't keep
you from their schools and humour or historical
secrets once you have the keys – parents

or no parents.

I found you there, fending for yourself in quiet
corners of that kiddies' cage, puzzling over
puzzles with infinite pieces missing. Pieces with
ripped pics and toddler-gnashed knobs. Pieces
that were never there in the first place: the wee
price you pay for donation. But you pit your wits

anyway, sharpen your tools on the ones we
share, lean as half-sucked candy, when really

the tongue has more to give.

18

Jayla

Your identity is dependent on a strip of masking
tape, a cramped straggle of lettering, lost in the
chronicle of you, leaving your history behind.

Where did the narrative begin? And where is it
now? We recite your name back to you, listen
for your muffled thrum, the mute corrections

you throw back at our pigeon rhythms: the tinny
burr of our untrained lungs. Our stumbles make
you laugh. You opt for connection

over correction

and we like you too.

19

Najib

No one said it was macho to paint
but you can't stay away: how the
colour melts and drifts from the
glut of past, page puddles of
diluted stains that make
everything you do
more pleasing.

20

Hanin

Your name means yearning, craving, tenderness and love. You get to be passion pure, all wrapped up in a five-letter lovechild of a label: a Proto-Indo-European parcel still sat on the shelf

unpacked

expectant

anticipating the life you've been born into, an appetite for so much more than is given. And it's not greed.

It's not grudge or malice or envy of any kind, gutsy girl – but a straight-out hunger for growth, a hankering for what is possible when you peel back the skies and watch the blue drool hope all over your world like folds of raclette. None of

this

was ever meant to be permanent

so you make the best of it, no holds barred. You mirror everything we say: words that meant nothing to you last night are now nattered back and forth between these four walls, no doubt

in my mind: you'll be fluent by Feb. We float
from *I spy* to *What's that?* and I watch the pride
in your pa's face as Deutsch fires from your
infant jowls, Alu fully lost in a thrill of sounds he
gets none of. Just the normality and peace

in your play, where time stands still:

the grin and bow in his hands

that mean thank you.

21

in the flood

brave is boarding a blow-up boat with your flesh
and blood bound for the belly of the sea

leaving your house, home and elders who
wouldn't make it past the porch

relying on tricksters to lead you bleating to the
Promised Land

dragged through mountain mines 'n' deathtrap
dens, the dregs of rebel fighter drones

it's hiding under trucks and trains and time-
warped containers stuffed with poundshop shit

no one really wants to buy

trusting the hands of strangers who talk in
cryptic, pagan tongues

it's feeding hollow mildewed cheese to your
child 'cos it's the only bite on tap

living back to back like prepacked sardines and
pestered by desperate yobs

wanting to work but can't because, because,
because

it's being shunted from bundesland* to bundesland until someone finally yells stop

being told you can stay, play the game but take your foreignness to the grave

being told you *can't* stay after nine months' transit, 'cos they've booked your flight today

brave is heeding to humility when everything is ripped from under you

it's believing the body, when the mind understands nothing, a land you barely know

i say you're brave but you just see "evarb" when the mirror tilts your way

afraid, you say
just afraid
all the time

evarb didn't save your dad or mother, sister or brother

and now it's just us here, a fistful of words, both signing sorry

22

Tirana calling

Two tribes span the girth of the room. They are
new and silent with no strings attached, and
their attention cleaves the chaos

neat asunder.

And it is chaos. A class with no roll call. No rules
or course books or record sheets: my clan
coming and going when the Bundesbark

deems it's time to hit the road –

a Ferris wheel of love and no arrival. Just a
hustle of papers and appointments between
that mean yes or no

cambered across the skyline.

You take what you can get. There's no wisdom
in this, all these deadlines that really are dead
for some from beginning to end

line for line

whole tribes hacked in half according to age
and health and livid flips of the wicked. But here
is hope, wefted across the centre space like a

tight rope they haven't learned to walk on.

23

Teaching turns into a two-hour yoga workout I
could be better dressed for, switching between
floor and wall, wall and floor, drenched in
ambitions they don't share. I'm on overdrive.

They're on overload, beginners head-banging
against a curb of flames. And if I took a moment
to look inside, I'd see that I'm burnt too: my
body howling at me to stop, slow down,

go home. But I can't,

hoping they'll get the grammar if they stay just
five minutes more. Hoping they'll learn to love
the lingo if I scrape my mind raw. *Je pense que
ça suffit pour aujourd'hui*,[1] Samid shrugs

in his usual modest way, tearing me out of my
trance. He's right. Of course he's right, I nod,
hasting my words to a halt. I notice each face in
turn, as if for the first time, each fixed hard

on me

here. We are silent for the longest second ever.
Toi, tu es fatiguée,[2] Samid says, telling me what
I'm too weak to admit. To me. To them.
Teaching without tenses after ten hours'

translation. And next time I set the alarm.

24

Julia

I beam at the list with Julia's name on it, the
guard gnarled by a curiosity I refuse to soothe.
Nothing, I wink when he asks which, why, what
on earth, the pry in his eyes I want to keep
where it is. She's more help than she knows.
Everything about this is better shared:
situations and snags neither of us have known.
We observe. They observe. I learn to teach

all over again.

We divide up our skills into tents of knowledge
and pool them somewhere in the bottled space
between. We pull out our straws and dip in
when we need, a place too tight and safe for my
ego's bloat. No time for hearts to bust or bleed.
Just humour to keep the show on the road. And
I know I'm lighter when she's there, two steps
forward and one back without. Grateful fast

becoming word of the week. Gallant. Roguish.
Bowed about the body of someone I need to be.
Quicker than I can be it. Last time, we brought
rage to the table, a spittle of feelings breaking
rank with our code, the slaver of life we couldn't
leave behind 'til we're guests in our own house.
Her hand now planted on my anger saying
sorry. I say sorry. Then we open the garden
door.

25

Then, there were cracks, rifts and signs screaming at me to get the hell out, home no longer home with our drugged-up houseguest slobbed in front of the TV day and night, and long outstayed his welcome: white, wasted and far too spoilt for his own good. Fugitives everywhere I turn. And now rage fleshes itself out inside of me, compassion hanging by a thread of perished rubber bands I can't help

stretching.

My monsters want blood. My monsters never know when enough is too much. We can never agree on terms. We can never sit down at the same table and pretend we like what we hear, the lives we've always wanted to live, the friends we're unable to share. Still resisting the me I long to be, while protest drives the show. And maybe I haven't understood just yet: it's not the flat that needs to change.

26

More faces. Eyes open as fishhooks. Expectation packed from wall to wall, swollen as sturgeon roe. How many elephants can you cram in a mini? We're about to find out.

There's more lust than fear in the room while they're itching to learn, baker next to banker, stone mason next to software stud, a clutch of hopefuls who've never picked up a pen. Ferhad

fills his book backwards with A to Z and 1 to 10 when we're not looking. It's probably his first. He grips his pencil like a harpoon in the name of hand control. And I've lost count… how many

times we rearrange his fingers each week, rewire the frail tendrils of letters that drool into a snare of hieroglyphics three lines south. He learns by ear, illiteracy filing down his senses

scalpel-sharp

and he spits words back at me the others can't get within a mile of. No catch. No tear. There are things the mind can do when you leave it be. There are things words will change forever.

27

We need teachers, translators and therapists. We need the fruit of multiculturalism, the unwanted bloom of migration hiked up on the spice shelf 'til now – as if diversity were the worst that could happen. And it's times like this

we notice when our bread is buttered. It's times like this we learn what give and take really means, and that no one took more than they gave or gave more than they took. And if we remember to rub both sticks in synch

we might just pull off a fire.

Demand outstrips supply. There are volunteers of every kind. Just not enough. The cops put out a call for Farsi, Pashto, Igbo, Albanian, the four favoured forms of Arabic. Flavours of the month.

The police pay well. Reliably. Punctually. And there's a heap of work to be done – from delinquent endeavour to deportation plots. The Polizei always finds a way to get what it wants. And for once, it's not English floating the boat.

You do as you're told. You erase originality from every case you undertake. Another name on the registry board. Another weight on the social welfare wall. Individuality has its place somewhere, a very long way away.

28

The alarm clock jams when I hurl it halfway
across the room. It's thirty-two minutes to eight,
my willpower grounded by a skeleton of lead
I'm not in the mood for defying, as if my age left

me

long ago. It's cold beyond the covers. Outside,
there are emails to be answered and notes to
be written. There're people who ask too much
and those who ask too little. There are needs I
ignore and truths I can't bear the sight of. And
there's a shadow cast across the breadth of my
turf when I haven't slept enough. This is often.

This is too often.

Answers I can't access when guilt takes the
reins, the way it whips every last strip of
physical wisdom from my bones, my brain
hungry for unconscious paths before the REM
of me implodes. *Soldier on*, it says, buffing me
about the ears, branding my tiredness a sign of

original sin

transposed to the realms apathy. Something
like burnout I haven't seen coming. In fact, I
don't even know I'm burnt. Just a little bashed
about, my body carting me around like a bruise
                                        on the move
that's forgotten where to go.

29

Life is looking up with Pessoa in tow. A page or three a day to keep me sane. Tagging along at hip-height, just a strap and buckle away from

escape.

The houseguest is now gone. And I'll bet Pessoa had a hand in it. Never a word too many. Never a word too soon. Like he's massaging the mind's eye – every last vessel – from lash to lid, duct to gland, cleansing the mucus of myth and self-lie, shielding in a membrane of charm.

And maybe it's a better way to ward off bugs as autumn takes a plunge, Fernando fighting what wildfire can't contain in this hall that's not a home. Not a real one at least. Numbers rising. Temperatures falling. People camped on raw stone in their hundreds, queuing one on top of the other for loos and baths and meals that thwart the gospel of hygiene code. Arguably.

Off the record.

There're things I'm shown I can't unsee, the finest, littlest needles of reality. There to query. There to roast. Fibres of goodwill with only measured intent, the spirit of our annexed humankind that doesn't give away anything for

free.

My body awakes wrestling with something beyond the system, *the something* everyone's had. Though maybe it is the system. I gargle cheap vodka to keep the germs at bay, chump on toes of garlic and red-hot horseradish between vats of sage and ginger tea. I try to do the one thing I never do enough of: Sleep. I try

to keep on top of this. I doze between translation tasks, an arse-about-face irony that the work comes in when I do nothing. No social media. No self-promotion. Just place my head on the pillow because that's what I need. Later, I pack in a flat viewing and friends: friends who are lonely with families, their kids and chaos, the endless piles of laundry and toddler tantrums, the isolation of having no one to lean

on. And I only remember

to breathe

when I leave.

30

Sleep urges me to bind the group, the class too far now to start over every time a new kid hits town. Only guilt thinks otherwise. And it lays tight and weighty on my chest like the lurgies I'm grilling in turn.

At market, I dose up on avocado, blueberries and pineapple, my basket brimming with antioxidants and accidental bargains. I run into the woman with ginger dreadlocks who is everywhere and anywhere I go of late. We

share a friend and enough familiarity for a five-minute yak before our banter runs out. But she's candid and real and I'm perking up now. I buy a gözleme on the way for something to do. It tastes of flour and cheap oil. I throw half

and go home.

31

Rayan

After two years in Sweden, they sent her packing with unsat high school exams and five languages under her belt, her mother barely hanging on for the ride. *Why?* I ask. *Why not?* she says, slapping herself on the thighs, *who gives a damn where you are, when you're not a minor anymore?* All the friends and connections you've made, the new community and roots you have laid: all as ephemeral as ice in the Syrian sun. *They turn on you when you turn eighteen,* she shrugs, as I ask her age.

Rayan is brave. Rayan is wise. Rayan has a head on her neck that will save her arse. One day. Right now, it's just a nest she needs, pals and prospects in a world that never lets her keep them. She wants to study and thrive. She wants to train to translate, travel the globe on a safer pass – one that doesn't send her home.

The Swedes said it wasn't enough to be half Syrian when the warlords came. It was the Libyan bit they didn't like, the dad her mum divorced years before for bashing her in, the bare strength of the crone in her family's moon. Taking the moral high ground in some patriarchal farce 'cos you're only half-worth saving. That's that crux of it, the nuts and bolts of Nordic decency, running out of jokers.

32

Laura Poitras lights up the Bethanien panel. I've been waiting all week for this, nine eleven of the year. And although I'm often loath to plonk people on pedestals, there's strong evidence to suggest this woman bloody rocks! From data protection to national security, there's no art without activism or truth without hacktivism, no matter how hard you grit and bare your teeth. You can't unrelease the truth once it's oozed its lifeblood into our streams of consciousness, the facts and figures, tactics and triggers. You can't play angel once your

cover is blown.

But what kind of world do we live in where revelation is relabelled interruption: severance, interference, disruption? What kind of labs are there for that? What kind of lab rats, willing to swap exile for public lies, documentation for inner strife: a delve of rusty inquiry with only one logical score? This

is not a film. This

is not the drivel of some multi-media Adonis hell-bent on driving the box office bill. This is exploration. Stout. Unshaven. Not pretty to look at. The womb of art, skin-close, asking more questions than it is able to answer.

Yet.

Gestation in real time.

Growth in slow motion.

The Zeitgeist waiting for its moment.

33

Almost New Moon. I'm awake again at five. Restless. Nostalgic. In love. On the twelfth of September two thousand and one, I quit my mind-numbingly fuckwit job, jumped on a plane and left for the mainland. As shifty as it seemed. This is life. You leap. You land. You don't look

back.

Because you can't go back. Not even

in dreams.

Especially in dreams. Forward is the only way to find out what you should've done: what you shouldn't have done. Though when I look at where we are, two million refugees and counting, I find only recycled dice doing the rounds, the humanitarian spoils of their weighted intent. I find motivations from a sullied mind, ideals that don't tally with those of the displaced. And now my birthland wants to go that one step further and ban the blood of others under threat. The rigid sickness of this island's ills fills me with shame. I am angry. I am sad. The jagged arrogance of a barren soul that yearns for the might of Boudicca, the grill of barbarian hands. And I won't appease the spit of delusion, the gob of law and tug of war, like two thousand and one never happened – The same band of yobs who'd sell out the young, kill off the old, but fail to rip the European from me.

34

Chain reaction

I knew you'd dreamt about it, almost four thousand miles from the scene of the crime flames redcircling the centre of money. Now the epicentre of woe: fat nostrils of anthracite pandering to the gods like cheese-shaven walrus tusks, charred with grit and pain into some gargoyle's chops. I rang you, remember?

We got sent home an hour into the day. Made a beeline for the first bar to deal booze off the Edgware Road, sign-speaking to screens that made no sense. No words on tap to swallow what couldn't be construed. Nothing really strong enough to drown out the biggest bang of our lives.

It was the eighth day of a job I hated in the name of student debt, still scraping to keep the six-metre-square cell of a zone four bedsit, calling people who didn't give a fleeting fuck about you. I wore a tie like the boys were forced to do. And I mean boys. They wanted women who didn't speak like women, women with baritones in their blood. But women who'd still bark and bend and heel. Kinda barking up the wrong tree with me, my cv longer than my dad's by the age of twenty-three. And only the lad I lured in Strawberry Moons ever beat that. It was a phase. A long phase – where faking interviews turned out more fun than doing the damn job, the filth of owning brogues no more than a bloodless feat to keep up with those sworn in like a spasm of eel spit-fried in aspic

five years on. And I saw where this was heading, filleting my inkish life into flax seeds, impasse signs between my teeth. So I jacked in this shit on the 12th, as dodgy as it looked, and grabbed the first jet out of town.

35

On the other side of the street there's something like growth happening that can't be seen up-close in this civic cave, this parish hive: soured roof beams flaunting to the elements like a lumber of bone caught in the upshot

of its soul
                    before the squall.

It's been my mirror for months, as my tack descends into a purl of pneumatic groove, the band of stoned doves I've tried to keep hidden, but now cankering, tracted into the attic. For fear the whole house goes down.

I catch myself making fists again. I find nail marks the size of emoji signs whenever I fan my palm, and there aren't enough sheathes of skin to protect me from myself, the barbs of self-deceit picking at sticky flesh. I want to be

stronger, safer, swimming in the clear but I'm still watching from rooftops, bearing all in knee-high boots, not built for the climb. My right fist clenches into a walnut. I sleep like this every night of late and wonder why I'm tense when I

wake, my body bellowing what the mind won't hear. Over and over. Out of my depth. The answers written in my grasp. And if I press hard enough, I can pretend I haven't seen how anger spurs, intestine groping with the winds.

36

The group's going full steam ahead: We're on
to first conditionals and Albi's wolfish for more,
all fifteen years of him. He'd be *Abitur*-fit* in no
time if he got one to one. But I can't do

favourites.

And besides, I'm flagging, it seems, skiving
Sunday-night sessions so parts of me can eat,
sleep and heal, fighting not to show, fighting for
powers I spent two months ago in a bout of erg.

Julia leaves a note on the door. There's a hulk
of translation to tackle and I'm too bogged down
to do what I have to do, the flat contracting like
a house of cards around me. We're both getting

cabin fever. I take myself off to cafés to work:
to give us both space. To not make a big thing

of it.

It's not a thing.
Just a fact.

I spread myself about the city and take different
routes home. I get creative with escape, know
where and who to avoid when – among four
million. It's a fine line. It can get complicated.

Gambling's not for the faint-hearted. I win a
round trip raffle and turn it down: gundog

already bored by its catch. I knew I was going
to win before I did, laughing – the inappropriate

hit I didn't try to hide. But being stuck on board
with that co-winning cocksucker would've been
more torture than I could hack. So I fib and
blame it on my little bro's bash, the one

! haven't spoken to

for years.

37

Dad would've brained me. We've had regular words this past year and no one tells it straighter. I miss the flesh version that left too young. It's like I've only truly known him since he went. And the guilt of that never goes.

Though he'd back the education bit. I know he would: the earth I want to move by stirring minds, the hunger for people to learn themselves free. He'd have got that. He'd have got why Bora wanted more than Albania could give: sick of packing supermarket shelves instead of studies she had to quit for grain. €160 a month and no breaks. And I know he'd have done the same, seen through Albi's urge for school and skills he couldn't get back home: siblings smart enough to change the world. Just not there.

I'm trying not to get attached. I'm trying to just teach. But don't know how to *just teach* human beings who have run from harm and hypocrisies that keep them from their future. They're in my head when I shut the door at night, when the thrill of a coffee-time paper numbs the urgency of their pleas. My days

bathe in a bleed of privacy, an illusion busting out of the screen of life, a piddly word, not immune to connection. I cannot treat them like algorithms. There's no arm's length in a smile. No misunderstanding when cash is swept to one side. They want to see the city I see. They

want to be reborn.

None of us know where we'll be in three months, though I don't tell them this. I immerse them in fantasy, carry it in my bag, on my bike and shield them from facts that will wrench us

apart.

38

Refugee becomes term of the year. Everyone's talking about it. Everybody knows best, clichés spun nationwide from Freiburg to Flensburg, from swanky Berlin bars and Hamburg harbour to the backwater barnyards of Bremerhaven. The usual work, school, housing whine, when

nothing

goes your way.

The women lined up along the counter wear sexiness well in their fifties. I watch, listen in on their conversations with half an ear and replay my own with the other. They let their men spout bullshit before butting in and tearing out the ego from under them. It's the fags that give us more gall than we came with, sipping house whiskies to Bowie while the world beyond is imbibed by the Med. Cigarettes don't care about your sex.

My lungs make odd sounds on the dance floor these days. Maybe I've read too much Bernhard. Maybe I'm just suffocating myself between stress and sulphites, hoping that somewhere in all of this, there's a signpost

and solace,

and deep down,

a sense of peace.

I brush off a lover on the first of October. What a way to start the month. I coat my skins in Vaseline for anyone who clings too tight now, not knowing when to back off. I use the day for walking and writing, hunting down other loves instead. The town shrinks into a series of cafés and tube stops, where I can't keep still. Tempo escalating. Restlessness expediting. My tripled lives eager to just march on the spot to keep warm. At least the neighbours are nice.

39

The groups begin to thin. Volunteers with time on their hands do classes during daylight hours and keep our unsaid factions apart. Learning German becomes a homogenous job you can't

take personally.   I miss my mob, I'll admit.

But they need smaller, safer spaces to open their mouths. No room to grow in a gang of this size. No room for multi-ethnic ideals among the raw of trauma. There's always a logic behind loyalty, practicalities you wouldn't oversee in their shoes, as much as I wanted the mix, maybe even the dream: that this foreign tongue could unite the Levant with tenses not tension.

Letting go is my lesson in this, a change that frees me from the conscience I am sewn to, my own fears, my overloaded plate. The West Balkan gang becomes my tribe. When asked why they don't take daytime class, they shake their heads and laugh. Course they did! Every last one, from morning 'til night. *They took them*

all.

I bow my head in respect. My heart purrs at their commitment: to their learning, to their future, to the country they've sought inclusion from. Alma pulls out her phone and points to the word *privilege* with an infant's grin. *A luxury*, Albi nods, googling his mother's mind: Full-time schooling is the luxury they never had. And I read more pride than he can veil in his smile.

We're carving bookish out of bakers. Albi says they spend every second of non-lesson time slotted between multilingual shelves at the local library, submerging themselves in sounds that could sink or sail their status here. From the moment they rise, everything is done *auf Deutsch*, he says. *Obsessed*, Bora smirks. *Obsessed*. The folks she's known her whole life but never seen. The political odds they'd do anything to overturn.

Who the hell stamped Albania safe? she snaps, her parents' hard graft lost to callous racketeers, profits rotten into a skein of life that wasn't worth the bother. Armed bandits running the wild, wild west of their Balkan score. She speaks six languages but won't finish uni with 2000 Euros a year over her head and three years to go. I tried

to find mentors. I tried to play the CSR card: Bright young minds with new knowledge, the key to tomorrow's world. But no one bit. Just biting lips at a prejudice I can't ignore. No one cares about flair with the wrong passport.

The ugliness of this gets left outside the door. Here they exist. Here they are real, humans surfing on the warmth of connection, not the wave of a sieve. For two hours three times a week, they can leave conflict behind, the fights

over showers and soap and fresh bread rolls,
the thieving and bullying they turn a blind eye
to, looking after their own.

Bora tries to stay useful in the eye of the Amt*,
bides her time as interpreter for muter tongues,
for tour guides and doctor meets. Anything to
make herself indispensable. Anything to keep
to her clan. But there's nothing I can do when
the Home Office signs her deport date: another
fool discharged like a whore when her service
stint is done. Just in time for Christmas.

Epilogue – The Bundesgott

They said only good things would happen if you prayed to the Bundesgott*. There'd be food and shelter, and above all, life. Good or bad. Big or small. But life away from bombs, brown boots and the slew of bile you called home.

So I hung an eagle in the corner of every room where my laughing Buddha would've been. I missed the Buddha. It was harder to smile at a bird of prey, its penchant for stamps and stars. The Bundesgott takes things so damn

seriously: Eighty years on and still the same gut-wrenching relics of the Führer fisting out of the front page on a Sunday morn: Lucid syncopations with Mahler and Freud we call culture, all live and well. The Süddeutsche[1]

does us proud. The Bundesgott has a healthy love of poetry, reels 'em off word-perfect from the pit of glib constitution: trophy of the tax office, driving force of job and housing centres, a bedrock of psalms with just one very long

corridor.

He tunes his day to tepid laws, code after chord of deviation and inspired whim, the guile of raving ambiguity – where the rational has never looked so irrational around the rule of thumb. Except for him.

Though he likes me. I've seen. I've seen how he hangs sneaky mug shots across a bounty of tiles, fingerprints as bittersweet as child's play, shuffling his flavour of the month. We won't call it control. We won't call it clout. Something

like love with neat conditions. Never meant to swallow too soon. All those ghosts of the past. The luck they tried elsewhere. Anywhere but there. There, where the trains took a one-way track. Then a wrong turn. Once upon a time.

In the land of the Bundesgott, you can snooze on the streets, no fear of hotshot rocket-love. No lesions for loyalty or traffic light warnings for lust and war: grand gestures we've agreed to pay for. An A-1 bleed we like to call

denazification. And he won't marry. Not for love at least. There's no Frau or Herr Bundesgott waiting in the wings. Just a melt of fetish, dark and worldly, drooling in the flesh, fanning his polyamorous arse. Come one, come all.

I ask for his protection. It's the first time. Before I thought it was just a god I needed. Any god. Anyone I could find inside. But I was wrong, and grandpa right, as I await goodwill: You may stay. You must go. Long after La Manche[2] has

parted.

You become a believer. You! Heathen! Leave your pagan years behind! Hallelujah! Praise the lord! The Bundesgott loves you. Even if he didn't love your Opa or Oma[3] and gnawed the rest of their kin to ash. You jump in, take a front

pew.

I got why pa ground his teeth at night, perhaps why I do the same. They braced high seas to swerve the Bundesgott, from Brno and beyond to the Dover docks, the rounds of mutant alopecia, the non-existence meant for them –

until they found each other. In nothingness. Had kids and grandkids who came from nothingness, who became the fear they had run from: the inheritance that sucks, until someone shouts STOP. Enough. Make peace with this

monstrous piece of past that's more mine than not, too rank to be real: hard to see in this place that boasts home in the nest of my now. And when I think about it, aside the guilt of ambling free: without the brute of history's yield, I know

there'd be no me.

Is it ok to be grateful? Just grateful? I mean, how many had to die for me to exist? Defining myself in a world where fear is less of a foe, when you know where it is. There. On the surface. Turn your back while the AfD cackles.

The Bundesgott sent Oma packing with prerequisite recipes for Sachertorte,

Pischinger[4] and Rahmspinat[5], the good housekeeping guide to perpetual exodus, home always out there somewhere, simmering

on the tip of your tongue. I remember how she spanned the strudel dough to twice her body length, yanking back and forth with her scrawny limbs like a battery-powered Hampelmann.[6] I wondered at the violence of her thoughts to pull

it off. Her Apfelstrudel[7] never failed, loose gloop flying between her palms, taut as falcon wings, just inches from level ground: the skin of a Shar Pei rippling the air with gamma rays. The scent of home infusing walls, stifling the musk of old

recycled bags. It took years to see the self-love in that, respect pervading the palls of trauma, the eye teeth of a mass murder machine that still chatter in the distance, far, far off at the dearth of remorse, whenever the voice shies.

History is seared into my heart but doesn't have to close it. I choose. Do the opposite. Make my home in the hunters' den. And then help others get there too. An exile for an exile I earn fair and square. No special favours or systematic repay,

this gift from gramps. Rehousing the past. Resetting the present. I take the path of most resistance, baton in hand, my birthland now a breeding ground for the same. So much senseless self-harm drummed into my DNA, hushed, unconscious and so virally fertile, it must be easier to just never change. Options, options, whilst I've been Brexited. De-Britained. Another blow from those who hail difference and divide, unpicking the stitches

as fast as we can thread the eye. Old angst they've padded along the way, while we get burnt, spiced up, something like splintered inside our fibreglass lives. Until we are sand. All of us. Run a finger through and we become

one.

Glossary

Foreword

AfD: Alternative für Deutschland, the largest German right-wing party

Chapter 1

warten Sie bitte. Warten. Wir bitten um Geduld: Please wait. Please be patient.

Chapter 4

Toastbrot: Processed sliced bread for toasting

Chapter 6

1 *Staat*: State
2 *krank*: ill
3 *Auf Deutsch*: in German

Chapter 10

haben und sein - Verbs "to have" and "to be"

Chapter 12

Kommune: municipality

Chapter 13

Bundesländer: Federal states

Chapter 16

1 *AfD*: Far-right political party: Alternative für Deutschland (Alternative for Germany)
2 *Fressen! Ficken! Fertig!* : Eats, screws and leaves

Chapter 21

Bundesland: Federal state

Chapter 23

[1] *Je pense que ça suffit pour aujourd'hui*: I think that's enough for today.
[2] *Toi, tu es fatiguée*: You're tired.

Chapter 36

Abitur: German A-Levels

Chapter 39

Amt: Public office

Chapter 40

The Bundesgott is a word I created to express the exalted, seemingly arbitrary power of the political elite. Literally translated: The Federal God.

[1] *Süddeutsche Zeitung*: a national newspaper
[2] *La Manche*: English Channel
[3] *Opa or Oma*: Grandpa or grandma
[4] *Sachertorte* and *Pischinger* are traditional South German / Austrian pâtisserie
[5] *Rahmspinat*: creamed spinach
[6] *Hampelmann*: Jumping Jack
[7] *Apfelstrudel*: Apple strudel

Acknowledgements

Firstly, I'd like to acknowledge the courage of anyone who has either attempted to, succeeded in or succumbed to the mission of reaching asylum elsewhere in the world, not to mention those who have had to stay behind and endure severe conflict and crisis.

A big thank you to everyone who has supported both me and the project in various ways: to friends and family for your loyalty and love, to my laid-back, turkey-talking flatmate Hubertus for your up-front stance, to my classroom sidekick Julia for your solidarity and sense of humour, to Fran Lock, Fatemeh Shams and Andy Croft for reviewing *Federal Gods*, to Culture Matters and Caparison Books for publishing individual poems from the collection, and last but not least, to Palewell Press and my dedicated publisher Camilla Reeve for your invaluable time, insights and commitment to putting *Federal Gods* into print.

I'd like to add a special thanks to my students at Rathaus Wilmersdorf for teaching me vital lessons in reality, humility and trust. I learnt as much as I taught – So, thank you.

Biography – Clare Saponia

Clare Saponia is a London/Berlin/Brighton-based writer, poet and coach, and the author of two further poetry collections: *The Oranges of Revolution* (Smokestack Books 2015) and *Copyrighting War and other Business Sins* (2011). Clare's poetry has featured in various magazines and anthologies, including *Smokestack Lightening* (Smokestack Books 2022), *They want all our teeth to be theirs* (Culture Matters 2021), *The Cry of the Poor* (Culture Matters 2021), *The Brown Envelope Book* (Caparison Books 2021), *Witches, Warriors, Workers* (Culture Matters 2020), *Kakania – An Anthology* (Austrian Cultural Forum 2015), *The Robin Hood Book – Verse versus Austerity* (Caparison Books 2012), *Emergency Verse – Poetry in Defence of the Welfare State* (Caparison Books 2011). Clare also works as an artist, translator and teacher.

Palewell Press

Palewell Press is an independent publisher handling poetry, fiction and non-fiction with a focus on books that foster Justice, Equality and Sustainability. The Editor can be reached on enquiries@palewellpress.co.uk

Lightning Source UK Ltd.
Milton Keynes UK
UKHW021825080522
402647UK00005B/155